Arise from Vapours

By

Jean Pagano

Rick,
Remember to see the
Beauty in everything...
Peace & Long Life

"Finn"

authorHOUSE™

1663 LIBERTY DRIVE, SUITE 200
BLOOMINGTON, INDIANA 47403
(800) 839-8640
WWW.AUTHORHOUSE.COM

First published by AuthorHouse 03/09/05

ISBN: 1-4208-4089-4 (e)
ISBN: 1-4208-2924-6 (sc)

Library of Congress Control Number: 2005900923

Printed in the United States of America
Bloomington, Indiana

This book is printed on acid-free paper.

Acknowledgements

Arise From Vapours is a collection of passing scenes: journeys, reveries, woodland hymns, and observations, blessed, hopefully, by the Muse. In the days when the prophetess sat at Delphi and inhaled the fumes from deep within the Earth, visions and exhalations were delivered to both she and those that consulted her for a view into the Otherworld. While I did not have access to the mysteries at Delphi, I tried to impart to paper what the Muse showed me in my soul. I hope you enjoy this first collection and that it gives you a glimpse into a world apart

I would like to thank the many people who have made *Arise From Vapours* not only a work in progress, but also a chronicle of the things I have seen. To the many people who have read my works over the years and given me their thoughts and suggestions, I thank you. To the people who inspired me to write, I can never thank you enough. To my mentor Michael, I send you my Irish blessings. To my parents, who always encouraged me to do more, I thank you every day. To the Gods, from which all things arise, I honour you always

I want to give a special thanks to Ginger Meeder, a truly great poetess, for her encouragement and gentle readings of my poetry. Thank you to my photographers for gracing my pages with your wondrous images of beauty: Rosemary Ashby and James "Finn" Hamilton.

Finally, to Newelle, you are in here too, my dear

Dedication

To the Muse in her many guises

Table of Contents

Chapter I
Journeys

Ashen Way

The swirling voices surround me
And warm me on this cool evening
Fire ablaze
Moon on the wane
I pause to reflect

Sullen ashes
Brushing the waves of the nearby lake
Softly tracing the surface of the water
Sighing, with a ripple
As they write the future
In moonlit undulations

And I float
As light as nothingness
Into their rustling care
They place upon me
A subtle enchantment

The branches in this night's light
Teased and twisted in a magical haze
Gently surround me
Caressing my face
No longer heartwood,
Nor branches
Nor leaves
But hair
And skin
And warmth

As the wind arises
Sweeping sideways
Across the water
I feel that soft brown hair

Touch the sides of my face
My back against you
As I rest my head
Against your torso
Your arms, your fingers,
Hold me entwined
As each whisper of wind
A promise, a prayer
Does hold me enrapt

Water maiden,
Ashen-daughter
I feel the firmness of your body
Holding me from behind

I feel the energies,
Mingled,
Coursing through my meridians
And also through yours
Your branches
Your fingers
Moving rapidly before me
Signal Ogham
And my future unfolds

You tell the tale of worlds in passing
And notch away years
And mysteries sublime
So close to the Seeker's soul
A kaleidoscope
Of trees and seasons
All speaking in voices
Resplendent of seeds
And flowers
And thorns

Jean Pagano

Touched by the Goddess
And Springtime in motion
Moved by the God
To the fields and streams
You show me tomorrows
I never imagined
And also todays
As yet unborn

And I am enveloped
Inside of you now
Search for the centre
The heart of the matter
You take me in completely
And show me the key:

I arrive at the crossroads
With an ash at each passage
Twenty-five tree-lined roads
Radiate from the centre
And at the end of each passage
There are twenty-five more

Arranged as fibres in a web
Thus are all possibilities described:
Each and every contingency -
For at each joint in the collection
Exists the potential for any event
Under the guidance of a glyph

For as the Ogham, these runes
Are interrogated for information
One tumbles headlong down
A tree-lined passageway
Looking for an insight,
A stopping point on the grid

This then is the nature of the Ash
I yield to you, O Mighty Tree!
Standing up so tall
To scratch Ogham across the sky
Roots reaching so deep
Trace Ogham through the earth

If one were to examine closely
All matter in this world
One would find the glyphs
Inscribed on ev'ry thing,
Composing ev'ry thing,
Becoming ev'ry thing

And as all of the world runes
Condense into one single metaglyph
The world vanishes into mystery
Moving rapidly before me
Signal Ogham
And my future unfolds

Jean Pagano

The Muse, Anew

The call of trees,
Birch,
Rowan,
Ash,
Has taken me
From the grips of
Electricity
Into the forest again

Inception
And beginning
As the light began
To grow
The Muse whispered
In my ear as the
Solstice sun did wax
Goodbye to the old year
She said
As she stirred my soul
For my first word was the
Tetragrammaton

The quickening did
Follow
As strange visions
Abounded
The Muse touched my hand
But she was not to be seen
"You will see me in your
"Dreams", said she
"For the other world
"I will reveal is not just
"Reverie,
"But the Other side"

And I began to grow
But not of cow's milk
Did I drink
But nourished yet
As the ewe's milk
Began to flow
My next word was
Divined

Then,
Ere Spring
Came the floods
To wash away the former
Time
To soften yet
The bed for planting
And as I looked up
Through the forest
I saw all
History
Written in the branches
And as the rains
Streamed
From those branches
I saw the Great Ones
Hanging there
From limbs
The water-bodies
Form-ed
All letters of the Alphabet
The Muse did show me,
Still so early,
Through darkness
Yet the ciphers shone
All letters of the Alphabet
Engrossed
Was I to such
An extent

Jean Pagano

I barely felt
The waters grow
From 'round my ankles
'Round my waist
'Round my chest
'Round my neck
In my nostrils
Over my head
Everywhere
The Muse did lift me
Over water
Kept me from the flood there
My next word was
The sound of tides
Rising

Then to drive the
Water away
The fire-branch
Did heat the day
Cut, it bleeds the
Crimson-flow
The fire does
Burn
From within
To heat the land
Now fertile
Where the water
Has soaked the beds
Of seeds
The fire will provide
The flame to grow
As I looked up through
The trees
No longer did I see the
Rain
But 'stead saw fire
As Sol did shine

To warm the gentle
Earth
And then the Muse, anew
Did place her hands
Afore my eyes
"The Fire is to feel", she said
"The Fire that burns
"Into the Soul
"Into the Earth
"That starts the dance
"From seed to flower
"Should never be seen with
"The eyes
"But felt with warm
"Embrace"
And with that the Muse
Did surround me with
Herself like pod around a seed
Like bark around the alder
My next
Word was the ember-glow

As I looked up
Next
Through the trees
The Moon I saw
Betwixt the branches
Bringer of the morning dew
There I made my
Home
The wicker cottage
Kept me warm
As dew was found
On the wall outside
The Muse did take
Me by the hand
And show
Enchantment

Jean Pagano

To this bard
And taught me
Verse and wonderment
And show me growth
In Spring's bright
Wake
From water
To field
To dew
To light
I saw there under
Darkness turn
Into light
Into brightness
And felt the rush
Of growth
Within
And as the God
Did then withdraw
His time, for now,
To be exchanged,
He brought us from the
Inner warmth
Through death,
Through stillness,
Through coldness,
To germination,
To this place,
And as the Goddess
Came to rule
A season
And a quarter turn
Past Yule
The Muse did take
Me to that tree
And taking all my
Clothes from me
And wiping all the

Dew from me
Took me in her
Took me deep
Took to where
The seed does grow
And said as she
Engulfed me whole
"This is the
"Ecstasy
"Of growth
"For now I'm in you
"Evermore
"I will your first lover-be
"I will your best lover-be
"I will provide sparks
"For your soul
"And turn emotion into words
"To put upon your parchment
"There
"And I will love you
"All your life
"And I will be your
"Wicker-wife
"And I will be here
"Long and past
"The time that you
"Forget me"
Her body soft
And supple-warm
Her limbs like branches
Held me there
Softly swaying
The dew did cover
Us both then
We danced beneath
The May-Pole then
And bathed in dewy
Sensuality

Jean Pagano

I felt the verses
Swell within
And thanked the
Muse
Again, again
And we made love
Again, again
My next word was
The Muse's name

Directly after ecstasy
The Muse did clothe me
'Neath that tree
And said these very words to me
"Though now you of the
"Pleasure know
"And many verses
"Will arise from our
"Encounters
"Here and anon
"Yet sensuality
"So sweet
"Is only part of emotion
"It is intense
"It causes one to lose
"Perspective
"As personalities and soul
"Commingle
"Yet the other side
"Is there
"As well
"And yield emotions
"Intense
"As well
"And you shall
"Experience these
"And learn the pain
"That denial brings

"And when you've
"Learned your lesson
"Well, we'll seek rejoinder
"Then again
"This is a portent
"Of future time
"When you'll forsake me
"And forget me then"
Though I protested,
Quite in vain,
The Muse did leave me
There and then
Be ragged, bedraggled
I chased her then
Through thorny thicket
I cut myself
Time and time and time again
'Till blood was all around me
And as I wander through
The thorns
And recollected times
Now gone
When I danced naked
With the Muse
The poetry of sorrow
Swelled
Like an ocean in my head
The parchments sang
Of sorrow-sweet
And I remember
Better times
And looked
Forward
To meeting her once
Again
My next word was the longing

And when the longing
Went away
The Muse was there
Again
To form me like
An Oaken tree
Tall and straight
Hard
Unyielding
Arms like branches
Outstretched
And beckoning to the
Gods above
No longer did she
Take me by the hand
But held me firmly
By the shoulders - true
And then she said to me:
"For I have taught
"You of the Ways
"Of light and water
"Love and denial
"And of the alphabet
"Yet now the time
"Has come to feed
"You the
"Acorn of Knowledge
"For you to see the
"Dark side,
"The side that is hidden
"You will be safe from the
"Mundane
"The issues o' the world
"Will bounce from of your shield
"And you will feel your
"Roots go deep
"To seek the knowledge
"Underground

"To tap the reservoirs
"Of millennia past."
I begged the Muse
For comfort still,
To frolic in the
Springtime lawns
To abandon clothes
And cares
The Moon, the Moon
To dance upon
She stayed my hand
She kept me clothed
Her voice was loud
By her lips didn't move
And as her words
In my head resounded
This is what she said to me:
"The time to carry out
"Your training
"In the ways of the
"Olden ones
"Is here now:
"Don't deny it!
"I will protect you
"And we will frolic
"Later on
"Stand firm
"And learn the lessons
"Which will strengthen
"You now and anew"
So down went my roots
To seek rejoinder
With the knowledge
Hidden deep
As knowledge
Entered into my roots
The need to tell the world
Did grow

Jean Pagano

For ev'ry idee
Ev'ry notion
A acorn did upon me grow
My next
Word was the seed

Then one day
The sun shone overhead
A brilliant light
Through the trees
All was illuminated
All was aglow
As the power rose
And I did grow
In stature
In nature
In spirit
In wonderment
The spark of life
That the Muse had
Nurtured all the
Many months had begun
To flourish
As I looked around me
At the verdant fields
So full of life
I saw too
Power in the fields
The endless cycle
Of rebirth and redemption
The forceful green striving
To reach the sun
To reach the sky
I too, like those plants
Outstretched my arms
Outstretched my hands
Through the sunlight
Through the forest

Through the treetops
To the sky
As I felt the
Heat of the sun on my palms
My power began to grow
And I did love my life
With all the power of my heart
And I did love the earth
With all the power in my body
And I did love the Muse
With all the power of my soul
For as she looked upon
My adolescence
The seed had taken
The boy did grow
She did embrace me
Softly, lightly
A summer's day
Devoid of wind
She did seduce me
Subtly, smoothly
A summer's breeze
To tease the branches
She did entwine me
Briskly, quickly
A summer shower
Close around
She did engulf me
Wholly, totally
A summer storm
With all its fury
Then she did say
While she held me:
"You have the power
"I take it from you
"I do return it
"And ever will
"I need your essence

Jean Pagano

"To drive me onward
"You need my presence
"To create the world
"For I have held you
"Here at my breast
"To suckle inspiration still
"We feed off each other
"Each a compliment
"Not quite whole
"Without the other"
And with those
Words
I took the Muse
Her flowing hair
Her milky skin
And I did love her
'Neath the canopy
Of trees
I felt the power
Swell within her
I felt the power
Grow in me
I felt the power
Of the world
As we lay beneath
The holly tree
My next word was
The power

After all the loving
Comes the warmth that
Wisdom brings
Knowledge of the joining
Two hearts
Two spirits
The Creatrix and
The Creator
After all the loving

Comes the warmth
That satisfaction
Brings
All is at peace with
The world
The Sun has thawed
The Earth
And then
The Water fell upon
The Earth
And then
The Fire rained upon
The Earth
And then
The seeds did grow
And as I looked up
Through the trees
I saw the acorns
High above
And as the wind
Did blow the trees
The acorns fell
Into the ponds
And sprouted
Universities
And as the acorns
Fell around
The sound
They made reminded me
Of the Muse's voice
Amidst the trees
And this she then
Did say to me:
"You too are like
"The trees you see
"Though acorns not
"Upon your branches
"Grow

"But wisdom falls
"Between the words
"For those who care
"To see
"And it is evident to me
"How deeply do your feelings
"Go
"How strongly do you feelings
"Flow
"For me.
"Stay upon the path of
"Wisdom, now, and evermore
"And then you'll find
"That wisdom keeps you
"Better then
"The pragma of
"All other men
"And I will always
"Be a-round
"To keep you company"
And I did then
Embrace that tree
Acorn-laden
And close to me
And then I felt
The presence of
The Muse, anew
And then I danced
Among the trees
And basked in the
Warmth of the
Mature Sun
My next word was
A thought

And now the forest
Full in bloom

Full in growth
Did sway around me
In all its glory
All Nature at
Its most creative
I sat next to the
Blackthorn
And I began to write
'Though all I saw around
Was the vision of the Muse
I felt her warm caresses
As my quill began to write
And write
And write
The reams did flow
I felt my creativity grow
With glory Sun
And Muse to guide
I felt as though
I'd write forever
The dream coalesced
Before me:
A tome of works
Dedicated to the one
Who gave me inspiration
Who fed my quill,
My thought,
My soul,
My empty hours
Under the sky
The Sun did dance
Above me then
The days stretched
Many hours long
The visits from the Muse
Were fruitful, long,
And passionate
Then, one day,

I noticed that
The days and
Nights grew similar
In length
And breadth
I asked the Muse
To explain to me
The waning of the Sun
And this she said to me:
"Worry not, of Sun
"Or Moon
"Or season
"Keep to your work
"The Wheel will turn
"The mundane passes
"As a veil before your eyes.
"The Seasons turn
"Around you now
"Like Sun above
"The canopy of trees
"Your work goes
"Forward
"Even though the
"Light may be diminished
"Let not the flame
"Of the inner-glow
"Go dark and untended"
And with those words
She wrapped herself around me
Like a whirlwind
And brought me high
Above the forest
To see the circles
Spin above
I saw the Sun
In its circling
Of the skies
I saw the Moon

In her many phases
I saw them come
Together then
In that nineteenth year
I saw the whole
Scheme,
The interplay
And grasped the
Universe in motion
And saw all things
At the same time
And learned the
Omniview
And then
In forest I lay again
The trees swayed
Quietly above
The Autumn kissed
The forest-face
I kissed the Muse
And wondered then
My next word was
The rune

And then the leaves
Began to fall
And only pine
Retained its green
And greenest leaves
Yellow and red became
In that harvest time
The weather
Cooler grew by night
While days became
More moderate
I looked upon
All that had
Become

Jean Pagano

And felt a sense of
Awe
The seeds that sprouted
So long ago
Came to fruition
In their time
The poems started
Long ago
Had fallen into
Rhyme
The Muse
My friend
Stood by me still
My how much did come to pass
She'd gone from mentor
To protectress
To creatrix
To my friend
To my lover
To my inspiration
Yet, there was more
To be revealed
I helped her with
The harvest tasks
To sow the seeds
Of long ago
To take the
Inspiration then
And channel it
And make it flow
We set in order
All the forest
Cleaned around
The changing trees
And once again she
Looked at me
Brown eyes
So earthy

And so wise
Again she said to me:
"For we have shared
"So much these days
"Perhaps more than you'll know
"We shared the sky
"The sun
"The trees
"The forest home
"Where we can grow
"For now to gather
"Is the task
"To rein in all
"We've loosed
"And store for
"Next time
"What we've learned
"And carry on
"Again, anew" ·
And I did take
Her by the hand
And walk beneath
The quiet pines
I did embrace her
Then
Again
As all the forest
Watched
Again
And as we walked
In silence then
I hoped we walk
This route
Again
My next word was
The gathering

Jean Pagano

Beside the forest
Yet still within
Did lie the
Part of reeds
The Muse did meet
Me there one day
As the veil
Between the worlds
Was thin
For minutes,
Hours,
Days,
It seemed
No word was whispered
No sound to hear
The reeds did rustle -
They rustle still
The Muse,
The reeds,
And
I
The Muse did rise
And walk about
Circles, circles
Ever wide
She always
Came back
To the spot
Where we had
Set us down
And then she
Looked at me again
A look I never shall
Forget
And with her
Eyes
So very brown
She did then look

At me and say:
"The time has come
"Author,
"Lover,
"Friend,
"For preparation
"For when I'm gone
"For now the year
"Has turned again
"For now the
"Dark Time is at hand
"The space between
"The worlds is thin
"I must soon bid you
"Fond adieu
"Until we meet again.
"For every word
"We've ever shared
"These words we'll share
"Again
"For every caress
"We've ever shared
"These too we'll share
"Again
"For every embrace
"We've ever shared
"We will embrace
"Again,
"Again
"For every passion
"We've ever shared
"We'll walk that
"Path
"Again, anew."
And with those
Words
A buck appeared
With antlers

Jean Pagano

Great and wide -
She touched
The buck
He dropped his head
All letters of
The Runic Tree
Were writ upon
That noble head
She touch him
Once again
And then
He raised
One leg
And lowered then
And then the Muse
Was gone again
Gone again, anew
I looked upon the
Forest
Then
The mighty arbours
An army still
And as the
Darkness covered
Me
I did prepare
For life without her
My next word was
A sigh

And then 'twas
Time
To carry on
Continuance
Did rule they day
The empty branches
Elders bare
Did scratch against the sky

And now the Muse
Was gone from me
Into the crack
Between the worlds
The Sun, of late,
Was colder still
A pale rider
Against the sky
I did wander
Far
Those days
Into my forest
Into the forest
I looked at all
The stages
Of the growth
That I had seen
I was a babe
When I first
Walked in here
I've grown to
Manhood
By and by
The Muse did
Guide me
The Muse did
Feed me
The Muse did
Love me
By and by
And now I must
Wait for that
Season
Coldest of the
Turning wheel
And I must
Introspect correctly
And carry on

Jean Pagano

And carry on
The spheres did
Turn again
One quarter
Winter did
Arrive again
I watched the
Season change
That morning
Watched it change
Again, again
All about me
In the forest
Did die that day
Again, anew
And all the Earth
Was cold and barren
Nothing stirred
Nothing grew
I went into my
Shelter then
To recollect
To introspect
My next word was
The dead of winter

And then the
Day without a year
Did come to me
In that Winter-time
The Wind was cold
But the days were longer
Changes come around
Again
And then I looked
Behind me
A fleeting glance
Out of one eye

I saw a younger me
Approaching
Trace the circle
Path again
And when I thought
To watch the
Sunrise
Up to the door
I did then go
And when I looked
Into the forest
There she was
The Muse, anew
And then I
Understood
That circles
Always come
Back
Again, anew

Apparition

All stood about
In a circle
Looking towards the
Central flame
As introductions began
And names and affiliations
Floated in the air
I saw her near to me
I looked at her, again
She was attractive
Her long hair
Blended into the dark night
That surrounded us all

I listened with curiosity
To the names and places
And stories
That traveled
'Round the circle
And waited for
The moment when
Hers the tale to tell:
First time at this festival
From West Lafayette
Her name floated by me
Without registering in my memory
I resolved to ask for her name,
Later...

The central fire
Near our encampment
Was crackling with life
And intensity
As the drumming began,

Drummers and dancers
And spectators, too
Flocked around the
Fire

The fire orchestrated
The rhythm and dancing
With the wood providing
The score
Ancient arboreal
Yearnings released
Through the flame
I saw her near
The drummers
And as she approached
I noticed her lithe
Shape
Her slender hands
Her softened corners
She then removed
Her shoes
To begin the
Evening's dance
What were the
Connections
Her soles did make
With the ground
There?

And I was enthralled:
After thirty-seven years
I had felt myself
Become
Uninspired,
My heart grown tepid
From disuse
And lack of ***intensity***
My soul anchored

Jean Pagano

In the mundane
A gale would
Not founder me
But the movements
Of hands and hips
And fabric
Enraptured me
I felt a lightness
That I had missed:

Lost so long ago.
I felt a joy and
A longing
Which slid me into
A reverie
Of rhythm, fire, and sound

"Here, play this"
And a maraca
Was thrust into
My hands
I played this
Instrument
Like I was
Carrying a
Fragile egg,
Still enthralled,
Still hypnotized
By the dancer
Who so caught my eye
"Shake that thing!"
And the egg turned
Into a rattlesnake
Which darted to and fro
Attacking the fire
And dancing to the flames

And at last,
The fire calmed
And the drums
Did lose their fury
The snake,
Now empty of venom,
Did fall unused
To my side
The dancer,
My dancer
Sat on the ground
And seemed to just
Enjoy the fire

I took a chance
And smiled in her
Direction
Perhaps she smiled, too
I thought about approaching
Her
My shyness
An albatross around my neck
Held me in check
The fear of rejection
Kept me a prisoner
Where I stood

And suddenly,
Slowly,
She reached for her shoes
And I panicked
Still held in place
By fear
By lack of courage
I so longed to speak to her
To gaze upon those
Soft lines
To trace them

Jean Pagano

Like an artist
Her feet slid into
Her shoes
Each movement a
Workshop in graceful motion
She looked my way
Once more
Grabbed her bag
And walked away

The snake in me
Still had some life
As I darted around
The fire's edge
I sought the light
From her lantern
I wanted to ask her to
Stay awhile
Longer

The light from her
Lantern
Was engulfed by the darkness
And she was gone...

As I searched and searched
From campsite to campsite
I could find her no more.
My nascent longing,
So long a memory
Was now a seeker as well
As I gave up
My search for her
For the evening
I vowed to find her
The next day

The morning brought
The light
Soft,
Slipping around
Corners and
Peeking behind
Trees
And search
And search
For the next three days
Each face
Examined
Each movement
Questioned
She was nowhere
To be found:
She *was* gone

I have since
Resolved to
Seek again
This apparition
To follow this passion
To worship the
Rekindling
Of wonder

To cherish
The reawakening
Of desire
I have lived too
Long in the
Lumberyard
And now seek
The company of trees
For she was
The birch seed
The whisper of

Jean Pagano

Potential
For she was the
Goddess
Incarnate
In <u>my</u> presence
She became the
Rowan
And symbolised
Conception
And changed
Into the ash
Upon her disappearance
To symbolise
Frustration
At my letting her
Slip away
One day
I will walk in
Her forest
And mimic
All her movements

Apparition:
Let me join you
In the dance
Of mystery and
Enchantment,
Next time...

Jean Pagano

Change of Pattern

Change of pattern,
Change of course
All things in their own time
And then to rest

So long the journey
Endured
So far the path pursued
To reach the crossroads
Upon that day
When frustration ruled
And all of time stood still
Perched upon a moment
And a decision

So slow the trail
So tenuous and true
From what was only
A starting point
Unto this day
Frozen in time
Move like ice flowing

For once the goal was plainly in view
Obscured by desire
And years
And time
And loss along the way
So much sacrificed for so little
In the end
For this too, I had to laugh

For in the journey,
Honour bound and duty clear,

A new tomorrow to be found
A new self to be discovered
Around that next bend
Over the hill beckoning
We offer our own legs
For the gallop of a horse
We offer our own limbs
For the rustle of the trees
From without we strive
To find ourselves within
And here again, I pause
In the end
Only peace desired,
Yet Discord and Decay
Define every shadow
Darken every day,
Where I thought to find
The caress of a Goddess
A sword presents itself thus:
To discover the heartwood,
One must hew away the bark

My armour, friend and second skin
I cut thee away,
My helmet, my face to the stars above
I bow thee down,
My shield, eyes to the day dawning
I drop thee away
My spear, voices of the Gods I seek
I lay thee down

I stand therefore exposed,
All I had gathered
Now gone
All I had fashioned
Worn away
And time,
Clever companion,

Jean Pagano

You look upon me today
Like on my first day
Your visage unchanging
Your eyes clear and true

And I?
My hair begins to blend with the sands of time
My face furrows with the movement of water and years
My hands sacrifice their elasticity for a moment in the sun
My soul awaits tomorrow with an eye on the passage of days

I fit the yoke of the mundane upon my shoulders
And course my way down passages worn and true
Work the work of ages with a breath of the sky
Someday soon I will fly and fly
One hand on the earth
One passion wrapped in fire
One flock of hair singing to the wind
One moment washed in cold desire
The Gods are Gods of patience
And sign unto the Sun:
All their words create the song of days
And the sky expands with each shimmering note
And imbues each leaf with laughter and sound,
Blesses every breeze with patience and understanding,
Sings a song to every heart
Of coming into being
Holding true the course
And finally surrender
And coming into being once again

So too I sing,
As I join into the chorus
And understand the nature
And purpose in the world:

Change of pattern,
Change of course

All things in their own time
And then to rest
Again

Jean Pagano

A Canopy of Ashes

Weary the journey,
I look upon the field and sky
And see that is stretches forever
Clouds sing their ever-song
Laughingly
Knowing that although they may change
They will endure
If not in some other form

And here I pause,
By the Gods,
To see where I have been
Trace the long journey-lasting
Many a day
Many a year
Perhaps only today

For I have been running
Breathless,
Formless,
Tirelessly racing
Spanning the lands
Overlooking the world from heights
Almost beyond imagination
And comprehension
Pumping my arms and legs
Striving, stretching
To free me from my shadow
Always so very close
Running to my destiny
Still,
Barely out of reach

Until today:
Today, I drop the battle
Today, I sheath the sword
For at the end of each skirmish
I find so much less of me
So today:
Here I stand
Hands outstretched
Face uplifted
Rays from the Bright God
Layer upon my face

I hold my sword aloft,
An offer of supplication
To He Who Lights the Day,
And with a release
And a heart outpouring
The flames of the Fiery One
Alight upon my upheld gift
Irradiating,
Illuminating,
Making my sword unto the Sun
And with a brief glance towards my Past,
I send my missile soaring behind me
To all the places I have been
To all the battles engaged,
To all the pains and wounds endured
And I give them all the gift of flame,
Flame and surrender

From an offering of Fire,
By the Gods,
Comes a rejoinder of air to fuel the flame
Comes a laughter of smoke,
By the power of the flame
So is all the water sent away
Not a tear,
Not a drop to dull the fire's roar

Jean Pagano

Consume, O Divine Lion!
Take my past as an offering
To end the madness
Take it all,
And give me Today

All around the horizon
The fires rule the day
Eradicate the past
Confiscate the memories
Once etched upon my soul
Burn them all.
Burn them all away

And this is where I will build my home
He in the present
Unencumbered by the Past
Unenlightened by the Future
Just the Pure Moment
Served with sword and fire

I find me here in this canopy of ashes
No more to sing the Song of War
No longer a servant of the shield and arrow
With every step the grayness stirs
The ashes dance in the air
Where once leaves pirouetted on the wind
Their ghosts are now gray and ashen

And as I step forward
Into today
I know now,
By the Gods,
Now I understand!
That in the wake of the passing
A new world is being born
I must look towards the horizon
For the promise that is Today

Let me no longer a soldier be
Let me be a farmer
And cultivate the Present
Each and every day of my life
And honour the sacrifice and offering
Of Fire and Ash

Jean Pagano

Exile and Return

How strange the return.
My hair,
My face,
My soul
Now different.
How often I have wished
That I could touch that place
Again.

But life has changed.
Tumult:
There is no better way
To describe the upheaval
That I endured.
Yet, I survived:
Some parts more callused,
Others,
No longer tender from a
Long, slow heal
Show their scars,
Like my soul.

By the Gods,
The world has changed:
Many of the stones
That I was buried under
Have been removed
Or exposed as
Shadows –
Insubstantial

The clouds march by.
Steadily they parade
Past

They exist on their own
Level
They participate in a
Reality so close to my own
Yet separate
As I move through them
Around them
Above them
Sighted from afar
They bend around my universe
And continue on their own way
I soar above the
Surface of the world:
I knew I could fly,
If only I desired
My path,
Like the Spear of Lugh,
Directed,
Aimed,
Intent in purpose
As I approach

Yet, in someway,
I am afraid:
Afraid of the shadows
Which will greet
My arrival
Will they watch me,
Sullenly?
Will they move
Right through me,
Unknowing?
Or will they have
Substance and form,
And reach out to me?

I often saw my absence
As an exile

But perhaps that is a myth,
A pretty word,
A dream,
A parade awaiting my
Return
Where one world yields
To the fabric of another.
They seek,
They join,
They separate
And the old world,
Awaits
And I return:
No banner to greet me
No warm embrace to
Welcome me home
Only a new day
And the approaching dusk

O Darkness,
I have seen your face before
You swallow me up
And I blend into the moment

I am scattered.
I am diffused into
A world that was
A time that is
And a story becoming.
I open my arms
And step into the night:
Twilight, I am home

Peith for You

Departure,
As your feet leave the ground,
Your soul begins to soar,
As it was meant to do

Free of the fetters of
Earthly matters
Floating gently
Above the clouds:
You and yours
And the world at peace

I will think of you,
As you take to the sky
I will wave to you,
As the winds carry you away

A rune,
A promise,
A name known,
Discovered,
Absorbed:
This is
Peith for You

I will wonder
As you are carried aloft
In the night,
Held tightly in the heavens
A breeze will get you by,
And I will look to the East,
Longingly

Jean Pagano

Translucence

Translucence is the pearl's:
Perfectly round,
Borne of a single grain of sand
A world,
A focus,
So perfectly contained

Each pearl a vessel
Each new day,
Each new memory
Absorbs into the heart
Of the orb
Protected by light
Safe within enclosure

The centre radiates
With an ethereal charm
As it glows,
It grows
Each positive occurrence
Causes the pearl to expand,
A little more

And left alone,
The pearl retains its beauty,
Stores each recollection,
Forever more.
Within its opaque nature
Events,
Moments,
Embraces,
Remain alive and vital

The pearl is patient:
While no new experiences
May invigourate it
For a while
Or longer
It is always
At the ready
For some wonder to arrive

Open your heart,
And the pearl is ever waiting,
Open your soul,
And the pearl opens for you
The passage of time
Never dulls its beauty
The wonder of love,
Surrounds it like a petal,
Opening for you

Jean Pagano

Chapter II
Souvenirs

Jean Pagano

Bandana

I remember when
My bandana
Was like a
Colourful belt
Around the skirt
That was my hair:
Long and flowing
Perfectly pleated
Always changing with
The fashion:
Mini, Midi, Maxi
Long and flowing
That was my hair

I remember when
My bandana
Was like a
Peruvian snake
Around the vines
That were my hair:
Strong and resplendent
Hypnotically swaying in
The jungle breeze:
Morn, Noon, Dusk
Strong and resplendent
That were my hair

I remember when
My bandana
Was like a
A golden cord
Around the grain
That was my hair:
Bundled and gathered

Drying in
The morning sun:
Amaranth, wheat, and rye
Bundled and gathered
That was my hair

I remember when
My bandana
Escaped
One afternoon unnoticed
Shattering the continuity
Of days
And thoughts
And time

Escaped from my top
To the peaks of
Many others:
Snowy, sandy, barren,
Close-cropped, long and
Flowing
Most not needing enclosure

Escaped from a culture
Of Sunrise and incense
Smoke and fire
Invocation and supplication
Expansion and transcendence
High noon and the burning
Brightness overhead
Cool afternoon and the
Raising of the lights
Dusk and dust of evening
Rising
Stars and the firmament
Showing
Midnight and the heavens
Glowing

Jean Pagano

Early morning and
Collapse

I foresee when
My bandana
Will be a comet
Encircling the sky
Raining down meteors
'Round my hair:
Sparkle brightly
Shimmer the light
Settle gently into orbit
Into orbit
'Round my hair

Absinthe

Absinthe,
Je me souviens:
Memory
Snowflake like
Aimlessly
Aflutter
On the wind:
So many years
Between then and
Now
The touch
The feel
Still brush against my
Fingertips
The scent
The ardour
Still linger in the air
The taste
The texture
Still invigourate
My tongue now
The time
The passage
Still tick-off
On some clock
There
The mood
The mem'ry
Dri—-ft
So slowly by

Absinthe
Je me souviens:
A time when passion

Jean Pagano

Ruled the day
Time, unmoving
A rock-face yet
To move
Or to be moved by
All destiny,
Surrounded by a
Sense of urgency
And immediacy:
Tomorrow stood
Only to extend the
Ever-present NOW:
Today would never end

Absinthe,
Je me souviens:
I studied your
Topography like
An engineer -
I struggle to reach
The pinnacle of
Passion and experience
Isobars of youth and
Beauty notwithstanding
Traversing ev'ry
Plateau
Hand-holds upon
Every ridge
And when the valleys,
Deep and verdant,
Beckoned me
Like Mother Earth
To the womb
There too I
Traveled:
Caverns, deep pools:
Searching for the
Source

Absinthe,
Je me souviens:
Haze, the vision
Obfuscates -
Then living for
The NOW was not
Enough
When self-cognition
Supplanted the need
For passion
When the call to
Knowledge from the
Universe
Was louder than the
Whisper of the
Mother:
«Abandon-ye those
«Caverns
«Abandon-ye the
«Warmth
«For you have
«Wings and you
«Can fly!
«Fly away,
«Fly quickly -
«The Universe awaits!»

Absinthe,
Je me souviens:
My head is swimming
The haze of intoxication
Heavy, pressing
Outwards on my brain
This is not MY youth
But belongs to those
Who must explore
The depths of their

Jean Pagano

Own Desire
And their need
To heed some
Primordial call
To search the depths
Of another:
To these young
Minds,
I am an outsider
To these young
Bodies,
I am not welcome
This is their dream
Now
This is their
Discovery

Absinthe,
Je me souviens:
All of this comes
Rushing
Up to wake
Me from my
Reverie
It is time
To pass the torch
To the next generation
I envy all that
They will
Find
And touch
And feel
And taste
And wonder
To you then
I give these gifts:
A bottle of Absinthe
And a topographic map:

Use one to guide you
On your journeys
Use the other to remind
You of the wonders
That you found
There

Jean Pagano

Endings

Sad the day when endings come
The realisation that much has been for naught
Lines on the page
Yet no writing to be seen
Sounds on the wind
Yet no words are revealed
So much time passed
So much time wasted
The fields are fallow
And so are the hearts
The weeds have overtaken
All that grew here
The plough, rusted, in disuse
The horse, gone to greener pastures, too

Promise,
The working of the soil,
The nurturing rain
These components are not enough
For the seed may well be a stone
Without the intense spirit
The heat of being -
Such a loss,
To sow such a fertile field
Only to throw the harvest
To the winds

Who to know
That when asking the winds to blow
That the air would be borne
On tongues of fire
Scorching all that lie before
That every greening would be
Withered

Who to guess
That when asking the rains to fall
That the waters would erode
Any order brought to these broad fields:
Where there was order
And form
There is now only
The ravaged earth
Deformed and deranged

That I prayed over these fields so long
The optimist with his eyes closed
So many years, wasted
Plough the straight track
Coddle the seed
Revel in the growing
Plenty the crop
Yet, the harvest to waste

Maybe, I should have moved the mountains
From one site to another
The mountains would still remain
Raised me a temple from those stones
To glorify the old ones
Who are so very wise

Perhaps, I should have raised
Crops for the needy
Never asking for more
Happy in the shade and succor
Of green stalks
And the swaying of the leaves

But no, I had to shape the field
Cut down the trees that lived here before
Make straight the track
Channel the water
Tame the earth,

Jean Pagano

By just one man?
The folly, the hubris
I turn my head in shame

Better to sit beneath the tree
And watch the sunrise
And feel the wind blow
And taste the rainfall
Than to build something
So temporary and hollow
Form where no form is needed
Intent when the reasons are hidden

And now the plough rusts,
The seed sack is empty
Wasted, squandered
The grain never made it to market
I ground it into dust
And dust is everywhere
It layers the world around me
My hair begins to gray
From the dust that settles there, too

Each hectare,
Here,
Here, they begin to reclaim
For this greenery
Is sown by the gods
To fit their intent
And now I sit me down
Beneath that tree
Which I once cut down
To listen
To listen
To listen to the wind
From the west
And hear what tales it has
To tell

Stories of the gods
And of the earth

Find me solace in magic
The call of the north
I should have listened long ago
But I could not hear
Yet now,
Just one ear is on my head
And just one eye to see
From now on, I will be the stone
I will journey no more
But the world will come to me
I will be the discovered
Not the seeker

Let me be passive
In the scheme of things
Activity has brought a bitter harvest
I will let the world come to me:
Here I sit beneath my tree
All the world will pass by me
I will watch and
I will hear
Standing on one leg
One armed out-stretched
To greet the day
All the rest
Will blow away

All the rest
Will blow away

Jean Pagano

Desire

We lie together
Before the Dawn
I pick you up
In my arms
Like an offering
To the Sun

We both face
The awakening sky
The first rays of the Sun
Stream though us
And make us transparent

As we kiss
The Sun bathes us
In a shimmering light
And we are joined
Here in radiance
In the gathering fire

And we are consumed
As the morning miracle
Overtakes us
Basking in the new day
And the heat of desire

Allow

Let me hold you in my gaze
Let all your cares
Slide into nothingness
I touch your neck with my face
I touch your face with my hand
I hold you like the morning sun
After the darkest of nights

I sense the catch in your voice
As you speak so softly to me
We wear our old cares
Like a faded shirt
So comfortable
And rare
We remember our travails
With heavy heart
And down turned eyes

Let me take that shirt
And put it out of sight
Let me bring the spark
Of love and wonder
To that ever-heavy heart
And take all of your worries
And put them in a jar
Expose them all to bright
Sunlight
And watch as they fade from view

Let me lie next to you
Like a whisper on a careless day
And wrap myself around you
Like a gentle kiss
As you awaken in the morning
Fresh and new to a smiling world

Jean Pagano

Let me open up all the blinds
That have kept light and life from you
Let me take you trembling
And keep you in my arms
And hold you safe from harm
Tomorrow waits unknowing
And unaware

But here we are today
Quiet and trusting in each other's care
Teach me how to sing
And I will sing this story
Again and again
Until the past can never
Find you again
Come sit with me in sunshine
And revel in the light of warmth
And care
Today
And as many days
As your heart can hope to find

Jean Pagano

Copper

Copper glows the embers,
Softly
Keeping the early morning
Company
Through darkest of night
And starlight overhead

Now the evening long
Passing
As the darkness gives up
Ownership
Of the endless sky
And the world all around

Copper, sensing the need,
Leaps
Outwards towards the horizon -
Empty:
Take the embers
And sprinkle in the low sky lacking

Copper is the dawn sky
Glowing,
Stretching from ember-seeded
Garden,
To reach out to the stars sleeping:
And the dawn expands

Copper is the Aube's bright colour,
Laughing,
Borne from out the ember-glow
Breathing,
Fire is the growing day's companion
Come from ashes, come to light

And I find myself in Air
Hands raised towards the solar disc
Shimmering
Colours stream from the light source
Divine
All colours distinct, all colours combined

And I find myself in Fire
Palms open to an Earth fire-centred
Molton
Radiating from a fire source
Divine
Warm the centre, warm the heart

And I find myself in Water
Ankle-deep in the streamway wandering
Onwards
Flowing from a water source
Divine
Flow the passing, flow, flow away

And I find myself in Earth
Boulders singing of an infancy gone by
Remembering
Echoing from an earthen source
Divine
Ever-slow the movement, ever-slow the time

Copper, and the colours surround me
Vibrating
Soft arms move to gently embrace me
Tightly
The heat of another presence
Stretch far 'cross the miles

The hues brush past me now
Surreal

Jean Pagano

The multi-coloured visions of this day
Ever-present
From early day to coming night
From dark to glow to light to fade

Copper is the mourning
Silent,
As daylight fails into dusk
Approaching
And imbue the fire's edge
With breath of flame again

Call to the dying day
Eternal
As life tumbles from sky to Earth
Timeless
To nestle in the fire again
As the elements dance sublime

All I Have Seen

All I have seen
By the Gods,
All I have seen

When I close my eyes
Today does not disappear
It just darkens
More

And when the Light is gone
And tomorrow is another
Battle
Fought with a flower
And not a sword
I look to the Sun
I look to the Sun

Jean Pagano

As You Lay Sleeping

Quiet and dark
Soft and subtle
As you lie sleeping
You dream of free flowing fields of rye
Grains moving like frozen water
In rhythm
In time

Sleep,
My love,
Sleep
Dream of better tomorrows
And the peace that resounds
In the emptiness of time
Wings flutters
And you dream of birds
Soaring high against the sky
Timeless,
Unmoving,
Evoking a memory of quietness
And calm

And I sit upon your bed
Lovingly,
And gaze upon your face
I see you have the face
Of an angel
And the heart of the sunrise
Always being born anew
I fold the wings upon my shoulders
And caress your face
And as my wings settle
Softer and softer upon my back
Wave upon wave

Of brightness and light
Move up and down your body
Flooding you in light,
In love,
In healing
Do you remember this feeling now?
Like a distant dream
Or the fragment of a memory so very long ago

Sleep still my love,
Do you hear the wind sighing through
Those fields of grain and memories?
Yesterday is just a dream,
Beautiful one,
And the pains of loss and loneliness
Are gone forever more

I lay beside you
Beautiful one,
And wrap my tender arms around you
And the brightness of light fills the room,
Fills the evening,
Fills your heart,
And then you too,
You do rise
And smile that smile meant just for me
And wrap your arms around me as we absorb into the Light

The gentle movement of wings
And the winds be passing
As you sleep away the night
My lips upon your forehead
And my wings around your heart
And you sleep the sleep of angels
So richly deserved
Light as a feather
Your drift away
Come fly with me

Jean Pagano

Your arms no longer tired
Your heart no longer heavy
Your heart is free to fly
Can we fly together, you and I?

By These Stones

By these stones,
I find myself again,
A man,
Without a home,
Without a presence,
A spectre:
Half of what I was,
Half of what I will be

What I thought was exile,
Was loneliness
What I thought was opportunity
Was exile
I have grown so cold,
That I trust no smile,
That I proffer no hope
In this dark world

Jean Pagano

A New Season

Blow summer winds,
Your breath has mellowed
Over time.
Gently the pages of history
Turn
New stories,
Twists and turns
Unexpected,
Sometimes unwanted
Present themselves as awakening episodes,
Potential chapters,
In time

Flow summer dreams,
Come into being,
Flourish,
And vanish again
Reabsorbed into the
Firmament
From which all things come:
The universe breathes
And life rises and recedes

Glow summer sun,
The heat and intensity of your
Gaze solidifies the
Process of this world
As things are baked by your glare
The histories are written,
Chisled,
Etched
On our minds,
On our spirits

Settle softly the sediments
Of life.
Yesterday's blossoms are
Today's promise of
Continuance tomorrow
As the past crumbles
I hold on to the essense
And fragments of that dream
What was,
What was to be,
What might have been
Only the Gods continue in time
All the rest passes
Panta rhei
Panta rhei
All is change
All is in flux

Meddle gently in the lives of others
Participating in the reality
Unfolding
To touch another
Brings reflexion to one's soul
The pearl of friendship
Held so firmly by the oyster
Of the heart:
Glimpse the beauty,
Touch the wonder,
Bask in its glow
Until the creature
Changes with the movement of currents
Unknown, uncertain
And the jewel is lost for now,
Perhaps forever

Turn the wheel of the season,
The new season.
As the Sun changes

Jean Pagano

Faces recede into the
Valley of the Past
I reach out
And my hands slip through
Those ghosts
As their images trail
Behind.
And I lament.
How can I hope to hold
Something that is not mine?
How can I hope to retain
A movement in progress?
We come together,
We flourish,
We distance,
We remember,
We come apart

Blow summer winds,
Drift me back on your warm breezes
Back to visit those faces
I once knew.
The present has the enduring semblance
Of eternity,
Only to crumble to dust and remembrance
With the ticking of the clock.
Lull me, tempting Wisps,
Caress me,
And the past
Awakens
And kisses me,
Gently

Blue Wonder

How different
Those eyes
Look,
Blue wonder,
Fearful
Dancing on the edge of
Polished steel
Keen
Fearless.
When there is nothing between us:
Clouds of smoke dissipate
Lenses,
Clarifications,
Obfuscations,
When all that remains
Is space between
My eyes of green
And your blue wonder
I can slowly
Feel your heart
I can begin to see your soul
Hiding behind
The story in your eyes
And when the truth
Is uncovered
And bared
You will gasp at the breadth
At the wondering
I will hold your heart,
Cradle your soul,
Paint the vastness of the
Azure in your eyes
Onto my story of years
And revel in the retelling

Jean Pagano

Until it becomes
Myth-like
And resonates
Like a timeless
Treasure,
Blue like azure,
Blue wonder

Chapter III
Hymns to the Gods

Aine Cliar

I came upon Lough Gur
That dusk
The Sun
A-sinking
Day soon gone

I came upon Lough Gur
That dusk
Unearthly fires
Abound
Around

I came upon Lough Gur
That dusk
To find a place
To rest my soul:

To eastern-end
I journeyed first
And saw a princess,
Fine and fair
Of pale complexion,
Golden-hair
She calmed my soul
With gentle breeze

To southern-end
I ventured next
And saw a mother,
Proud and tall
Of caring gaze,
Auburn-hair
She warmed my soul
With hearty fire

To western-end
I wandered then
And saw the mermaid,
Sleek and long
Of dreamy motion,
Ocean-hair
She refreshed my soul
With gentle rain

To northern-end
I weary-went
And saw the hag,
So drawn and old
Of ancient stories,
Grayest-hair
She shook my soul
With sudden storm

Aine Cliar,
I saw you thus
Was it a dream
Around the waters
Of Lough Gur?

Jean Pagano

Cradle

In a world of contradictions
And impossibilities,
Time and people
Rushing by in a blur of motion,
My life slowed down for an impossible
Moment
And I found you there

In the tangle of circumstance
And potential,
Your thoughts and feelings
Impressed upon my eyes,
Our lives intertwined
Over and over again
Never knowing,
Never *really* knowing
What was to arise

We met upon a plain,
Bleak and barren,
Our outer selves worn down by years
Of weathering
And shattered expectations,
Until all that remained
Was a thick outer shell,
Two standing stones
In a field of memories
And lost desires
Visited by countless
Birds and
Rains and
Time passing

Our once polished surfaces
Had dulled beneath the elements
Until we struck a pose unmoving,
Seemingly,
Frozen in time
And uncertainty.
Then, the interaction
Of wind and fire and rain and magic
And sound
Conspired to change the world forever

For stones we once were
And stones we shall remain
But beneath that worn surface
Pulses the energy of the Earth
Unbending, unmoving,
True
There are many wonders
That lie hidden inside:
The intensity of passion,
The turbulence of the retention of time,
And memory,
The ability to wait until our day will dawn
Anew
Heralded by Sun,
And Wind,
And Water laughing

And on that day,
The pulse will come
Slowly, deep, sullen
Emanating from the
Heart of Magic
We will begin to vibrate,
Slowly,
Each reverberating
With its own rhythm
At first

Separate
And then
Synchronise
Together
And we will sound together

Our outer shells will
Breathe
Like a statue come to life
How slow the motion will be!
Build to a crescendo
That only the Earth can hear
And then to pierce that morning
A tone will sound
Resound
Echo
And matter
Forming a pulse
Born in the heart of the Sun
Intoned by the dark magma
Singing underground
And then!
A tremendous din
Will tear our worlds asunder
And we will be reborn

And on my first day,
I will raise my face to the Wind,
To blow away the ages and crevices of the Past
And I will turn to face the Sun,
And honour the pulses of life unfolding
And I will wash myself in the Stream of Life,
For all life flows from the River deep and true
And then, I will sing the Stones
So that all the Earth will vibrate
And in this Circle Dance
I will turn to then face you

And on our first day,
We will sing to bless the Air,
Air, which blew us clean
And kept our surface
Smooth and certain
We will walk then through the Fire,
And purify ourselves in the knowledge
That adversity and pain
Disappear in the
Flames of Patience and Certainty
And we will forge the Waters
And rest safe in the knowledge
That Life flows around us
And through us
And above us
Awash in the tides
And we will never forget
The hardness of the Stone
Or the suppleness of our inner lives
Buried in those Stones

The elements are the cradle
From which we were born,
And formed,
And foundered,
And arisen anew

As I look upon your face
I see the benefit of patience
And careful understanding
And faith in the works
Of the Universe
So large
And
So wide
I cradle your hand in mine
And watch the sky go by

Jean Pagano

As Night covers us
Quietly,
Completely,
Absorbing us into the matter of the Universe
We merge into the future
We cradle our souls in this life
Together
And watch the sky go by

Early Away the Morning

Gift of song
In early morning hours
Swept by clouds of pre-dawn
Birds still slumber in the arms of the Aether

Planets move imperceptibly slowly
Overhead
Gracefully sliding through corridors
And passageways
Long since ordained
Sealed in precise starlight

The astral dance
Glistening movements
Only the Gods can perceive the beauty
And wonder
For the pinpoint lights of the vault above
Smiled in cold firmament
When the Gods were born
Who but to give them their names

The River-in-the-Stars
Flows slowly
Washes the cosmos
From time immemorial
Until tomorrow never knowing

Early away the morning
All the Earth looks above
And sees a whisper of motion
And a sparkle of light

Yet, when least expected
The arc of stars

Bends down
Kneeling at all Four Corners
To embrace the land
And impress its timeless form
On the spinning sphere:
A moving drop in a still ocean

The first bird moving,
Seeing the sky mating with the land
Lifts one wing skyward
And soars silently
Through constellations
And galaxies
And time
Living in the moment
Feathers do the Prophet make
Tell a tale of vast heavens
Sing a song of ambience and wonder
Early away the morning
Dawn arrives and blushes
As one wing greets
The gathering light

Avalou

From bare to branch
To Sun,
To greening
Leaf upon the tree

Avalou,
Sweet apple blossom
Open for the morn
Five petals do you present

Fruit:
Gift of the Gods
Redden,
Ripen like the Sun
A choice of beauty true

The cut,
So deep,
The sacrifice,
'Tis the time of the Season -
Hewn through the middle,
The skin yields to reveal
Five stones

From bare to branch:
The star,
An offering becomes

Jean Pagano

Evening Star

Dark horizon,
Trees brush the firmament,
Far and away

Night
And the flatness of the earth
Ebony is the land
That blends into the sky

Bright light,
Planet fair,
Green blue is your colour
A beacon in the night

Far out,
In the sea of stars
Afloat on a sky absorbing
Never-ending night
Engulfs you

So goes the dance:
Quiet finds the dark sky longing,
Somber is the void,
Until you rise again

Chapter IV
Another Green World Trilogy

Jean Pagano

Peith

Preparation
The journey to significance
The sound of air passing over wings
I set out alone

I set myself apart
On the journey to discovery
As I inhale
Warm the colours
Warm the air
As I exhale
Cool the hues
Escapes the air
Repetition,
The key to transcendence
I know for certain
Where the journey begins
But I am truly unknowing
As to the destination it seeks

As the rhythm of the breath
Becomes the backdrop for all
Reality
In this small world
I feel that the beat of my heart
And its timbre
Set the tone for the whole
Of Existence
For a small while
All that exists
Is the beating of my heart and
The sound of air passing over wings
It is the beginning of something
New

It is a voyage into change
It is a sense of a
New beginning
Is it the gateway to *feeling*
Or once again something
All too familiar?

I whisper a prayer
To the Gods
Hoping for transcendence
They hear all of the sounds
From the wearing down of stones
To the warble of whales
To the movement of the celestial spheres:
No sound escapes their
Perception
And I know that my supplication
Is not lost among the aether
And the mists
Riding high in the clouds
The beating of a solitary
Heart
The sound of air passing over wings

The search for something new
Perhaps a new beginning
Am I truly open to the change
That awaits me?
I open my heart and look for the answer
The wind passing by
Amazed am I
Gliding on the clouds:
A journey of transcendence
Will my soul be cajoled?
Will my body be caressed?
Who knows what awaits at the
End of the road

Jean Pagano

The road to the south
The road to heat and ambition
Smile in anticipation of the
Mystery
I should have known
The path to the Goddess
Is filled with mystery
And deep pools
Water *way* over my head

As I step from the clouds
I sink into the pool of warmth,
Familiarity,
And uncertainty

And when I arrive at the end of the road
Smiles and warm greetings will await me there
A home from home
Far away,
A sense of rejoinder
Far away,
Can I walk upon the water
To reach that distant isle?

Once arrived,
I will be feted with open arms
A welcome as though
No time has passed
No distance traversed
The pulse of life ever-beating
A few words of reconnection
And I will be there

Preparation
The trek is close at hand
I leave all my baggage behind
And I step into the unknown
Arriving only on a dream

And a shoestring
Dangled from a heaven undefined:
Pourous
Uncertain
Seeking wisdom,
Inspiration,
Intuition,
Gifts of a nature
Long forgotten
Yet promised to come
Again someday,
Today

The sun reddens my face
In preparation
Darkens my shoulders
And softens my heart

Anticipation is the rule of the day
What will I see there?
What will I experience?

I take one final breath
And step into an uncharted afternoon
Filled with the sounds of nature
And the slow passage of time,
The breeze on the rise
Synthesizing into a new sonata:
Anything is possible
As I step from the mundane
Into the edge of
Another green world

Jean Pagano

Another Green World

I Commencement

How did I reach this place,
I surely do not know
Did I fall from the clouds?
Did I glide above the water?
I stand upon the shore

The hint of salt upon the wind
Teases the edges of my hair
Salt and pepper
Salt and pepper
Wisps of hair
Dark little cirrus clouds
Upon a background of total azure
I stand upon the shore

I see the gulls swing so softly overhead
Lazily rising and falling
Like autumns leaves a-tumble
From a climate far from here
Drift, drift, rise with their own
Volition
I become the geometer
And seek the circumference
Of this verdant place

To the east, to the east
So the path does go
Walk to the Sun
For Sun is in abundance here
With each step
Another warm caress
My face is kissed by the morning glow

Kiss upon kiss
The glow of light washes my face
I am bathed in the light
Immaculate

I walk forward eyes closed
Relishing in the new found heat
Warm my skin
Warm my soul
Behind me
Each footstep upon the beach
Gently erased by the ocean
Not a sound
As any trace of my previous
Position
Gone
Vanished
Consumed
The ocean
A soft hand behind me
The more and more I walk
Eyes unseeing to the brightening glow
I no longer feel my feet into the water
As I glide along
Just above the surface of the water
Carried by the haze of morning
Carried by the warmth of the Sun

I become a vibration
Reduced,
Broken down into fundamental
Particles and waves:

Waves in the ocean
Waves in the sky
Waves we are as all things
And waves so am I

Jean Pagano

II *Discovery*

After having traveled
An arc of this island
The green heart of this place
Beckons me
Calls to me
The many leaves and trees and flowers
Wave to me from this point upon the shore
And now I journey inward

Between the shore and trees
A marsh presents itself
Quiet, still,
Sullen and mildly reflective,
The Sun rising just enough
To shimmer off the shallow waters there
With each step breaking through
The glass-like veneer of the waters
A ray is released to further brighten the day
Sparks fly with every footfall
And yet again
Each footstep
Absorbed
Erased
Forgotten

The trees swing shyly
In the slightest of breeze
Tease me as I walk their way
Seemingly uncaring
I touch their trunks
To *feel* their natures
To understand the inner workings:
Warm, warm their movements
Solid their foundations
A current,

A sudden electric,
Pulsating
An energy to behold!

My arrival in this garden place
Is heralded
By a gathering of hibiscus-buglers -
Yet it is the quietest fanfare ever to be heard:
They shake their bright trumpets at me
As I pass by the reviewing stand

The lizards scurry about
A blur of movement underfoot
For all must be in preparation
In this green place
In this green world

Bougainvilleas supply the colour
And flourish
To fill in the borders
Of this transition zone
Movement from marsh to dry land
Rocky, perhaps volcanic underneath
Who knows what the earth
Has been brewing
Deep
Deep
Under the surface

I encounter banyan trees here
Old, old guardians of this verdant place
Tree trunks rippling with age and wisdom
Guardians of this quiet realm

As far as I can see in either direction,
They form a line
Encircling the place that lies within
I touch them as I pass

Jean Pagano

Touch those waves of heartwood
Which have seen so many dawns
And I feel the undulations
And I sense me drift away

III *Repose*

The banyan wall opens
To expose a broad expanse
Of flowers, trees, and open spaces
In the distance
I see the blue waters
Shimmer once again,
That distant ocean mirror

Soft grass and calm winds greet me
In this interior world
The sun,
Just short of noon-day,
Hot upon my head
Speaks to me softly,
In warm waves whispering
"Sit you down here
"And rest
"Weary from the journey
"You must be
"Make this your home
"Home to dream in
"Home to dream of
"Home of dreams"

"Sit you down here
"And rest
"Ready for a new life
"You must be
"Make this your home
"Let me show you what will be
"Let me teach you of the wonders
"Let me bake you like clay"

"Sit you down here
"And rest

Jean Pagano

"Settling into a new form
"You must be
"Make this your home..."

And that voice does lull me
Like a distant recollection
Pulled forward from a past
Unbelievably deep

As the heat overhead increases
I feel my consciousness
Evaporate
Waves from the heat
Waves upon the shore
A never-ending undulation

I look above me,
The sky,
Vaulted,
A 360 degree view
As I see everything above me
I become the meadow:
I feel the wind blow over me
I sense the movement of vegetation upon me
I feel the warm glow of acceptance
From the Sun
All over me
And I am at peace

Gentle gusts of air
Caress me the better part of the
Afternoon
But perhaps an afternoon of Earth
May last a thousand days
And then the breezes stop
And all the world is still
And I awake

As I stir from my restful state
I see the continuity of this place
And feel a deep sense of quiet
Of peace
As the waves of heat rise from the ground
I am uplifted with them:
I find myself at rest

Jean Pagano

IV *Acceptance*

And here I find myself
Like a wanderer in a fable
Far from home
Far from the world I once new
Welcome to a new beginning
Cut from a new mold
Baked into a new form
Here
Today

Here I am the god of a new world
A world that is mine
Far from the crowds of another day
Far from the static and electricity
That so characterised my former life
I may not be able to make the sun rise
Nor able to encourage the rain to fall
But I may wander as I please
Unencumbered

I walk upon the beach
And stretch my hands to the sky
Call to the Sun
Blazing in the afternoon,
Red and vibrant,
I bow my head to a real God
Bright, burning,
Bringing life across the Universe
To here
Life, for all the plants to grow
Life, all the animals sing
Life, the waves washing upon the shore

As I raise my head
The Sun kisses my face

And I know that all is fine in my world
And I know that all is quiet in my world

I wander through the flowers
Their pollen colours my face
Their ardour courses through my veins
If I stand still long enough
Among the vines
As they come and entwine me

I will cease to be a man
I will be a *Green Man*
Part man,
Part creature of the woods
I will be as Merlin
In his wild days:
Glory in the knowledge of humanity
Bask in the feral wonder of another world
Another green world

I can run me naked through the meadows
I can swing me high amongst the trees
I can run and run at incredible speeds
Until the particles that make up my very being
Are scattered like a million grains of sand upon the beach
Carried out to sea
Evaporated by the benevolent Sun
Blown about in clouds
From sea to shore

Hurled downward
Accompanied by thunderbolt
To my island below
Absorbed into the green, green land
Wonder of wonder
Nourishment to a field of vines
Grown up among them
A face in a field of greenery

Jean Pagano

I feel the verdant pulse of
The rhythm of vegetative life
And I am reborn:
My skin no longer flesh and blood
But a synthesis
Of chlorophyll and fibre
Of skin and bone
Supported by a backbone made of wood

I am a product of this place, now
The visitor
The sudden guest
Become a quiet fixture
A part of this place
And here I find myself
And here I find myself
As one

The days and weeks
Merge into a collage
Of memories and experiences
I am one with the seasons
One with the trees
I rise and fall with the rush of the tides
The moon
The moon it lengthens me
Like a long shadow
When it begins to wax
The moon
That silver pool
It shrinks me microscopic
When it is on the wane

And so I live this life
A life of quiet
A life of peace
The only sound
The whisper of the wandering

The pulse of life
Among the green and growing
The shadow of the wing above
The slow cadence of the
Wind from the Sun
To be
To be
A part of this place
And here I find myself
And here I find myself
Alone

The thought occurs to me
I could be more complete
If I had another,
Like me,
To share this place
To dance the dance
And know the Sun,
The wind,
The sea,
The sky

The wonders I could show
To another
Another
And I begin to dream the dream
As I am entwined as the vine
I dream of another
As I leaf upon the tree
And flutter to the ground
As I fall
I dream of another

Let me tumble
From the tallest of trees
And drift for an eternity
To land softly

Jean Pagano

So softly
In the lap of the Earth
She will hold me
She will caress my shoulders
She will trace the lines on my face

Let me blossom
From the brightest of flowers
Pollen exploding
Resplendent
Each grain
Each seed
A beacon
A call for another
To settle in a fertile place
Waiting for a spore

A place of infinite softness
A deep, deep pool
I will dive down deep drowning
Only to be reborn
In the presence of another
Another
Another,
Like me

And then,
One day
Borne upon a slowly moving white cloud
Drifting by the Sun
Sliding over the shore
Landing in my meadow
Where I am but a blade of grass

Falling from the sky
Awhirl, awhirl
A pirouette of petals
Falling from the sky

Could it be a sunflower?
Could it be a rose?
Could it be?

I blossom and bloom the entire meadow
As the waves are quiet upon the nearby shore
The birds of the place fly higher and higher
To consult with the Sun
As I awaken from my dream
From the quiet
I see you there -
In front of me!

Your colour as white as the sands upon the beach
Your skin as soft as the highest of clouds
Your face - I saw it in a dream
As I awaken from my dream
From the quiet
I see you there -
In front of me!

Jean Pagano

V *The End of the World*

As you approach
The world moves so very slowly
It almost seems that you are not real
The setting of the Sun
Plays tricks on the senses
Everything merges in the
Coming of the night
Perhaps what I see is a shadow
A desire
A dream within a dream
And as I look again
I notice
You are real
I notice
It *is* you

My mouth forms words
Sounds I have not heard for
A long, long time
We exchange sensations,
Impressions,
Archetypal images across the many years
As our souls combine
A torrent of thoughts,
And sounds.
And vibrations,
Emanate from each of us
And bounce off of the other
I show you 'round my paradise
The hidden places
So dear to me
I could take you in my arms and soar
Off the meadow
Past the tree
Through the Sun

For you are here!
In this precious space in time
For the cosmos has today
Paused and let
Our worlds come together

We sit and dine
Close to the breezes
And to the sea
And the other flowers
And creatures that I had befriended
Come to pass our way

The words we exchange
Are merely echoes,
Reverberating impressions
Deep within us then
Deep within us over the many years
Reaching back untold lifetimes

As we wander about the island
We laugh
Through beaches and meadows
Paths and passageways
Past lizards and palm kernels

With the crimson sun in the West
We drift from place to place
Strange soldiers in a march
Across this place
Taking in the sights and sounds
Of this soft and gentle place

We finally venture to the southern beach
The south, home of fire and intensity
We remove our shoes
And stand amongst the waves
The waves,

Jean Pagano

They touch us
They strike out at us
They cover us with salt and sentiment
And cleanse us to our very souls

As you reach for my hand
I gaze upon the horizon
Looking at the brink of infinity
Standing at the end of the world

Who knows what is out there?
It never really crossed my mind
All that matters is
Here and now
Swept up in time

And standing side by side
Drinking in the fading Sun
Like a fine, red wine
Blending into the waves
Wind coursing through our souls
Gliding on through to an uncertain future
Yet standing arm in arm
At the edge of the Universe
Standing on the shore
Our lives to share
At least for this moment
Beneath the endless heavens:
Stars come rushing in
Streaking light
And life
And meaning
With the promise of tomorrow
And another magic day
Here,
In another green world

Departure

The joy of the meeting
Made sweeter by the
Eventual nature of
Departure,
Separation

As I arise
This final day,
Sky *so* blue and bright
That the greenest of leaves
Are aquamarine,
We go to the ocean
For one final
Encounter
With the endless
Horizon

On this quiet shore
We stand in the warm
Calm waters
Once again
Until the next time,
Until the next time

And as the waters
Recede
So does our time together
Rapidly come to an end
And the glow
And the promise
That defines our
Blue-green meeting
Slowly,
Slowly drifts away

Jean Pagano

The emptiness that
Anticipates your departure
Brings me back to the end of the world
The end of *this green world*

The waves come and go
Soft and salty
Warm and blue
Softly, softly
And with the repetition
You slowly wear away
Until all that remains
Are your footprints in the sand

And there I stand watching and waiting
Seeking some concrete feeling
With which to build a whole new world
A newer green world
But all that remains is a *feeling*
A feeling
A quiet joy
The gratification of meeting
Of sharing
And laughing
And touching,
Ever so lightly,
A feeling
A sense of the familiar
If only for a moment,
And then you are gone
Footprints erased by the ocean's
Gentle hand
Movement ever so slight
And then you are gone

I venture back to my meadow
Back to the trees
Back to ponder
That which has come to pass

I am left with a sense
Of peace and fulfillment
From an encounter borne of
Spontaneity
A quiet space in time

But the meadow and the sky
Unknowing of the transience
Of meetings and encounters
Continue on in their
Aquamarine glow
Pulsating,
Beating with a life
Uninterrupted

And I
I am once again the *Green Man*
At home in this green world
But something has changed
Subtle, whispered
Even the birds pull away
They fly higher and higher
Seeming strangers to this green field
And I search the horizon
For a hint
For a clue

I notice that the ocean
Still blue-green from before
Is moving further
Up the beach
Than ever before
Closer and closer,
So strange is the sight
As the water approaches
The banyans with their ripples
Are at home in the waves

And the water encroaches
So slowly on the perimeter
And teases the edge of the meadow
Itself
And then the sea touches my feet once again
Yet even more gently than ever before
I too, am borne away

I float out to sea
Towards the receding horizon
And look to my green world
Now covered in blue
The flowers from the meadow
Their stems grow and grow
They reach as tall trees
To the Sun and the sky

And as I drift further
I hear banyans laughing
In the company of my flower-trees
Rising infinitely high

And I float as on air
Through this ocean of softness
The Sun overhead
Overseeing the Way

A journey for tomorrow
Not knowing the outcome
But hope for the best
All along the Way
Search for the heart
Search for a like mind
A gentle touch
A slight caress
And the promise of
Another green world

Chapter V
The Seven

Jean Pagano

Glory

The glory of faith:
Believe in the best of life
Or believe it not

Orbit

Fate made the orbits,
Unending repetition
What is the surprise?

Rye

The taste of the rye
Sun and rain and grain combined
Smooth upon the soul

Gather

Memories so red,
Apples spilt from a basket:
I gather them up

Jean Pagano

Wind

Blow on, autumn wind
Through the branches, through my bones:
Did you cleanse my soul?

Ash

Tinder breeds the flame
Brightly burns all of my life
Only ash remains

Jean Pagano

One Ear

The crowd has one ear
Turn to silence, turn away
My voice stands alone

Chapter VI
Triquêtre Trilogy

Jean Pagano

Driven from Your Island Home

Soft, warm, ocean breezes blow
Gently slide away day to day
Sunrise often seen
Sunset just a whisper
But the days pass by
Like pages of a book
Blowing in the wind

Dreamlike pause
The space between the days
As one day drifts slowly
Into the next
Like leaves gathering on the ground
Until ten years becomes
Your autumn on this island

A conspiracy of moments
And subtle tragedies
Accumulated like old rainstorms
On your doorstep
A flood of happenings
A torrent of changes

Faces pass by and imbed themselves
In the solid passage of time
Lives in profile
Frozen in a time foreign and strange
Hands and hearts encountered
Always retain the warmth of touch
The walls that defined your world
Will forever decorate one part of your life

The breezes that filled your sails
So long ago as you hailed from distant home

Once your friends
Now your adversaries,
Your feet once barely touched
The ground here,
Now, with each step
A tree does grow
Roots sink deep,
Everlasting

For should you ever walk
Past that home again
It will always remember your name
Your presence,
Your key in the door:
Ghostly apparition
Forever spiral the staircase
Recall the schemes which kept you there

Child of the sun
Daughter of the waters
That ebb and flow,
How many moons passed overhead?
How often did the wind breeze past you
Silent,
Just a whisper
A quiet suggestion

And your dreams spoke to you then
And showed you golden visions
Of a cherished past in a land far away
And your dreams spoke to you again
And rumoured ice and cold and changes
Never anticipated,
Never welcomed
Each day, the walls called your name
Sweet as your mother's voice
Each afternoon, the garden promised you
Endless days in paradise

Each night, the seas whirled around
And evaporated the present
Leaving a blur
And a treasure chest of precious jewels
Masquerading as memories
Sublime,
Divine,
And the sands of time
Drained like teardrops
Into a well of sighs
And aspirations

What did you do there?
Told your story, I presume
To walls intent on recollection
To a world forgiving and absorbent
Lived your life in the moment percussive
A panting rain,
Herald of the change of seasons
And augur of the changes of life
Dampened your footprints
Left in lives and in sand
Preparing,
Like a sullen runic incantation,
This world for your change in posture

A gathering of birds circled overhead
And showed you wing and expectation
Telling tales abandoned by the wind
Scattered like an ocean of poppies
Red and succulent
Answer to no one,
Yet for that brief moment,
Your attention shifted
And your visions
And the envelope of passion
And intuition
Was breached and torn asunder

And all that was,
Became brittle and timeworn
And all that existed in the moment,
Blossomed, flowered, withered, and escaped
Upon a wind of forgetfulness
And all that was to be,
Shifted suddenly
The world was then a little less warm
A little less sunny
A little less familiar
And the spell was broken

Oh my dear friend,
To have lived so long in paradise
I saw you in your angel wings
Radiant, transparent,
Sheer against the sun

The song of change
Sung by a Goddess unseen
And even less understood
Intoned in a language known only
To the soul

The words took your arms
And lifted them,
And taught you how to fly,
How to carry you through the air
To a new and different chapter
Driven from your island home

Jean Pagano

Forbidden Fantasy

As I open the wine,
You are all around me,
And as I offer libation
You pour out your sparkling sensuality:
Gold and fluid.
I find myself foundering in your
Golden liquid state
You caress the sides of the bottle
Lovingly recounting the stories of birth
And planting
And endless sun
And harvest,
Liquid laughing
With the slightest hint of an accent
Mysterious, yet familiar

And as You are decanted,
Your secrets are all revealed
Moving from the vessel of structure
Into the flowing essence of being
With you, all is in flux
Changing, pleasantly aging
A constant state of irresistible maturity
And grace
Bottled in the fullness of suppleness
And beauty
Preserved,
Waiting,
Growing in flavour
Frozen in time and memory
And I see you there before me,
Revealed
I stand in awe of your golden shining beauty
And as I inhale your bouquet

I realise the depth of your mysteries
Firm and round
Kissed by the bluest of skies
And fairest of suns
You entwined yourself
Upon the vine
Turning and posing
On the outside
You are so beautifully formed
On the inside
Mysterious, delicate, enticing

As the nectar flows from bottle
To glass
The sound of your movements
Is pleasing to the ear
Round and glistening
It is the sound of your passion
Long dormant
And reclusive
Released upon a new and waiting world
Released to me
For it is the sound of dew arriving
It is the memory of storm and rain
And the rapid and desperate movements
Of the vine at the mercy of the storm
The fury of the storm at first alarms
And then releases the fearful soul
Trapped within the fruit of the moment
I dip my finger within the glass
Liquid yielding,
One touch and the body
Slides and ripples
Waves and waves of tension
And release
All from a single caress
Pent-up energy
Too long bottled

Jean Pagano

And now free to flow
Free to undulate
Like the rhythms of the oceans
Rise and fall,
Retreat and beckon,
As the wine moves round and round the glass
I am held hypnotic
Enrapt by your wondrous lines
Moving outward from the centre
Only to return
Richer,
Lighter,
Closer together,
All returns to centre

And from the tip of my finger
I sample the sweetness and delight
As your wetness liberates my tongue
And lets me know forbidden pleasures
Heretofore only imagined
Only shimmering as part of a deep and hidden
Dream
As I raise the glass to my mouth,
My lips taste your fruit for the first time
The golden promise flows and flows
Down my tongue
Arousing my taste buds as if for the first time
Awakening a hunger
A need
So long unfulfilled and forgotten
As the taste enrapts me
Like a dervish dance never-ending
I plunge headlong into the waters of promise
And savour the delicacy of your surprising nature
And the fruit nourishes me like I have never eaten
And the liquid replenishes a drought so long in lasting
I dissolve into you
I become the vine

Twisting and turning
You become the fruit again
Sweet and pleasing to the tongue
Firm and full
The story of all of life
Read from the tips of fingers
Awakened again
Never to sleep
Never to wonder
Secure in the knowledge
Of the mystery of the vine

Wisps

Goodbye, my friend,
Goodbye
The past,
Like wisps of smoke,
Disperses,
Separates,
And is gone

I am reborn,
With all the memories
To draw upon
Their weight
Diminishes
And they float away
Insubstantial

Today, my friend,
Today
I walk through life
Transparent
The wind blows through me
Unknowing
And free

I flutter like a shirt
In the breeze
Let the wind be my guide:
Arms open to the passions
Of the currents that flow,
Gather the air
Like a sail

Chapter VII
Arise from Vapours

Jean Pagano

Arise From Vapours

The heat deep in the Earth
Gives birth to the object of your desire
Arise from vapours:
As the mountain breeze
Skirts down stone and earth and slope
To infuse the breath of life
Into that form which waits
Quietly
Beneath the surface
Unknown to the world
A mystery even unto yourself
For you have *dreamt* it
For you have yearned for its formation
Deep within you
And by association
Then
Deep within the Earth

As winds dance, surrender in abandon
Exposing the surface as the earth boils over
Air and fire do not mix well without *intent*
The subtle interplay of elementals
Suggests myths without form, substance, or audience
But it is your *need*,
Your power to formulate that which is coming-into-being
Which ignites the spark that blends
The essence of air and fire into a greater blaze
Into the cauldron of gnosis
Wherein the corporeal mixture of
Divinity, gender, and persuasion
Combine to fuel the magic of creation

For he arises molten
With only air as his delineation

And the stirrings of desire
Whip and whirl winds around him
With which to give him fluid form
Man-child of the dancing fire
His first step is to experience the binding of earth
And each subsequent footfall
Brings his inner flame closer to the edge
Of solidity

Formed by the wind
As yet transparent in the light of the new day,
His streaks of flame and foundation
Colour him blond and auburn
Skin as smooth as the centre of the earth
Heart as vital and solid as our nickel core
His first wanderings take him to a small stream
At the edge of your great sea
For liquid fire is born in the depths
Of the great ocean
Where memory and the yearning to become,
To be,
To carry forward,
To blend again into the firmament
Are all neighbours in the Void
And as he steps into the water
Ever yielding, like your desire,
He becomes a form, a solid,
Accompanied by shadow and spirit
The clear and cold moistening
Give elasticity to that which was amorphous
Arise from vapours and climb into the skies

From a vantage point up high
He is drawn like an arrow to the place of his
Creation
Deep within you
Deep within the earth which is your double
He pierces you like the Spear of Lugh,

Jean Pagano

Never missing its mark
And as he passes through
You feel the emptiness
Result of your fertility
Result of your loss
You feel him beside you
Yet you may not see him
Because to you he is transparent
Without form or substance
Because you cannot imagine that
You have moved the world *this* way

The flame which tempered his soul
Passes through you
A vertical movement
You feel the heat of existence
And creation change the density of
Your very soul
As it passes through you
It invigourates your sense of
Touch and passion

The air which gave him shape and mobility
Lifts the edges of your hair and traces
Each follicle
Extending your sensitivity into the universe
Around you
Making you feel alive as never before
You are open and painfully receptive
To impressions and emotions
You may have never known before
But which are now etched on you everywhere

The dews which defined his footsteps
And led to a path leading under water
Glide over you, searching every pore
For knowledge, understanding, and emotive grace
As the water yields

So do you,
Giving way to the depth of true understanding
That every flower that blossoms in your mind
Will grow and flourish in the world around you
And that the magic you undertake will
Create the world around
And draw unto you the things you yearn for most

Arise from vapours:
Spin around you like the Mother's
Loving web
You create the pattern
You imbue the form with life and substance
One hand open to the Sun
One hand hold the Moon in obeisance
He blends into you
As you echo auburn and blond

Jean Pagano

Chapter VIII
Afterword

Anew Haiku

From afar a wish:
A night of peaceful dreaming,
Moon and stars anew

Index of Photographs

X "Flower", Page 131, By James "Finn" Hamilton, Charles Town, West Virginia

XI "Sky & Moon", Page 147, By James "Finn" Hamilton, Charles Town, West Virginia

XII "Author in Trees", Back Cover, By Rosemary Ashby, Auburn Hills, Michigan

About the Author

Jean Pagano has been writing poetry most of his adult life. He has been chasing his Muse for many years and has often found her an elusive quarry. The poems and haikus contained in this book represent the occasions where the world of the Muse and the world of the writer intersected and intertwined

Jean is a student and teacher of Runes and has worked extensively with the Runes of Ancient Ireland (Run Na Erenn Seanda) and the Ogham

This is Jean's first published collection of poems. His poems have previously appeared in literary magazines, small publications, and online poetry collections. Jean is a staff writer for the *Native American Press* and currently lives in Michigan

Printed in the United States
28321LVS00004B/329

9 781420 829242